EFFECTS OF MENTAL HEALTH

ANGER MANAGEMENT, ANGER DISORDER, DEPRESSION SOLUTIONS.

ETHAN HOLLOWAY

COPYRIGHT PAGE

INTRODUCTION

Anger is a strong emotion that can be triggered by feelings of irritation, hurt, annoyance, or disappointment. It is a natural human emotion that can vary from mild irritation to full-fledged rage.

What Are the Consequences of Unresolved Anger?

Anger suppression can be a root cause of anxiety and depression. Anger that is not properly expressed can damage relationships, alter thinking and behavior patterns, and cause several medical issues. Chronic (long-term) anger has been related to a variety of health concerns, including high blood pressure, heart problems, migraines, skin disorders, and digestive troubles. Furthermore, rage can be associated with issues such as criminality, emotional and physical abuse, and other aggressive conduct.

Chapter One

Anger Symptoms, Causes, and Effects

According to a Harvard Medical School study, about 8% of teenagers had anger disorders severe enough to warrant a lifetime diagnosis of the intermittent explosive disorder. Anger issues aren't only for teenagers, and it's critical to understand anger signs, causes, and repercussions if you feel you or someone you love is suffering from an anger disorder.

What Are the Different Kinds of Anger Disorders?

Anger disorders can manifest in people who have difficulty controlling their anger or who experience anger outside of their usual emotional range. Various specialists have presented contradictory lists of anger kinds, however, some commonly accepted forms of anger include:

- Prolonged chronic anger can influence the immune system and be the source of various mental diseases.
- Passive anger, which does not always appear as anger and can be difficult to recognize
- Overwhelmed anger is created by life expectations that are too much for a person to handle.
- Self-inflicted anger is directed towards oneself and may be triggered by feelings of guilt.
- Judgmental anger is aimed at others and may be accompanied by sentiments of bitterness.
- Volatile anger is characterized by brief bursts of intense or violent rage.

Passive Anger

People who are feeling passive anger may be unaware that they are angry. When you are experiencing passive anger, you may express your feelings through sarcasm, apathy, or meanness. You may engage in self-defeating habits such as skipping school or work, alienating friends and family, or underperforming in professional or social circumstances. Outsiders will perceive you as purposefully sabotaging yourself, even if you are unaware of this or are unable to justify your behavior.

Because passive anger is often repressed, it can be difficult to detect; counseling can help you understand the emotions driving your actions, bringing the source of your rage to light so you can deal with it.

Aggressive Anger

Individuals who experience aggressive anger are frequently conscious of their emotions, although they may not always comprehend what is causing their anger. Because dealing with real problems is too tough in certain circumstances, they channel violent angry outbursts to scapegoats. Aggressive anger frequently manifests as volatile or retaliatory anger, which can lead to physical harm to property and other people. It is critical to learn to recognize triggers and manage anger symptoms to positively deal with this type of anger to deal with this type of anger positively.

What Causes Anger?

A person's environment is a major source of anger. Stress, financial problems, abuse, poor social or familial conditions, and time and energy constraints can all contribute to the development of rage. Anger issues, like alcoholism, may be more prevalent in those who were reared by parents who have the same disorder. Genetics and your body's ability to deal with specific chemicals and hormones also have a part in how you deal with anger; for example, if your brain does not respond correctly to serotonin, you may find it more difficult to manage your emotions.

What Are the Signs of an Anger Management Problem?

Losing your cool from time to time does not indicate that you have an anger management issue. Anger disorders are diagnosed by mental health professionals based on trends in your behavior, emotional symptoms, and physical symptoms.

Emotional Symptoms of Anger-Related Problems

You may believe that the emotional symptoms of anger-related difficulties are restricted to anger, but other emotional states may signal that you are failing to cope with anger positively and healthily. Emotional symptoms include constant irritation, wrath, and worry.

If you are feeling overwhelmed, having difficulty organizing or managing your thoughts, or fantasizing about hurting yourself or others, you may be suffering from an anger disorder or another problem.

Physical Symptoms of Anger-Related Problems

Anger, like many other strong emotions, causes physical changes in the body. Allowing anger issues to fester can endanger your overall health. Some physical manifestations of anger-related issues include:

- Tingling
- Heart palpitations or tightening of the chest
- Increased blood pressure

- Headaches
- Pressure in the head or sinus cavities
- Fatigue

Short-Term and Long-Term Effects of Anxiety

Anger issues that go unresolved lead to anxiety, which can have long-term consequences in your life. Anxiety can cause dizziness, fast breathing, nausea, muscle soreness, muscle tension, headaches, and concentration and memory issues. Such symptoms might make it difficult to do regular chores and can contribute to a generalized sense of anger about life.

Long-term anxiety can be hazardous to your health and emotional well-being. Individuals who have frequent bouts of worry may be at a higher risk of having a stroke. Serious memory loss, chronic sleep disturbances, and relationship problems are all possibilities. Before your anger and worry wreck your life, contact me to find out what you can do to break the cycle.

Is There a Test or Self-Assessment I Can Do?

There are numerous self-assessment tests accessible online to assist you in identifying any anger or anxiety issues you may be having. If you take an online assessment, make sure it was prepared and published by someone who is known as an expert in the subject of mental health.

Even if the test is provided by a respectable organization, you should never use a self-diagnosis or an online exam to guide your treatment. Individuals who believe they may be suffering from anger difficulties should seek the advice of a professional counselor, a family physician, or a volunteer from a local healthcare organization.

Anger Medication: Anti-Anger Drug Options

Mental health professionals recommend counseling, group therapy sessions, and anger management classes as treatment options for anger disorders. In some cases, medication may help control emotions and chemical reactions in the body that lead to uncontrollable anger.

Anger Drugs: Possible Options

The type of drugs prescribed will depend on individual circumstances and take into account other diagnoses. Possible options include:

- Prozac or other antidepressants
- Benzodiazepines are known to treat anxiety, such as Klonopin
- Lithium or other medications are known to stabilize mood

Medication Side Effects

According to estimates, up to 50% of lithium users develop renal-related adverse effects. These effects are usually remedied by medical care or termination of the drug, but they serve as a good example of why you should only take medication for rage symptoms under the supervision of a physician. Other side effects of many anti-anger drugs include:

- Nausea
- Increased thirst
- Changes in thought patterns
- Fatigue
- Dizziness
- Tremors
- Fever
- Addiction

Anti-Anger Drug Addiction, Dependence and Withdrawal

It is critical to determine whether your anti-anger medication has the potential to be addictive. Addiction to the substance is determined by your personality, the chemical makeup of your body, and the drug itself. Discuss the risks of dependence and withdrawal with your healthcare professional, and make sure to strictly adhere to dosing directions. If you develop side effects, find yourself craving more of the medicine, or are unable to stop taking it, contact your doctor right once.

Medication Overdose

Always adhere to dosing instructions to prevent the possibility of medication overdose. If you have any health problems while taking the drug, notify your doctor right away because physical signs could indicate that your dose is too high.

Depression and Anger

Depression and anger are inextricably linked and can create a vicious cycle that is difficult to overcome. Anger outbursts can result in estrangement and feelings of guilt, which can lead to depression. Long-term depression can make it harder to manage emotions, increasing the probability of outbreaks of rage. Often, seeking professional treatment is the only way to break the cycle.

Dual Diagnosis: Addiction and Anger

Addictions to drugs and alcohol might impair your ability to deal with anger. It is critical to seek treatment alternatives that address both mental and physical concerns associated with your disease. A treatment program that addresses anger without addressing addiction leaves you open to future emotional disorders.

Similarly, attending a group to discuss your addiction without revealing your anger issues increases the likelihood that you may use drugs or alcohol to deal with emotional pain in the future.

Getting Help for Anger-Related Problems

Seeking therapy for your anger-related problem is the first step in regaining control of your life. Inpatient institutions, outpatient programs, individual and group therapy, and medication are all available as treatment resources. Learning about anger symptoms, causes, and effects will assist you in dealing with your disorder healthily and productively.

Chapter Two

Do I Have Anger Issues? How to Identify and Treat an Angry Outlook

Anger issues definition

Anger is a natural, instinctive reaction to danger. Some level of anger is required for our survival.

Anger becomes an issue when you can't manage it, forcing you to say or do things you'll later regret.

According to a 2010 study, unrestrained anger is harmful to your physical and emotional health. It can also swiftly escalate into verbal or physical violence, causing injury to yourself and the people around you.

Find out more about understanding your triggers and managing your anger in the sections below.

What causes anger issues?

Anger can be triggered by a variety of factors, including stress, family troubles, and financial concerns.

Anger can be triggered by an underlying disease, such as alcoholism or depression, in certain people. Anger is not considered a problem in and of itself, although it is a documented sign of various mental health issues.

Some of the possible causes of rage issues are as follows.

Depression

Anger can be a symptom of depression, which is defined as persistent sorrow and loss of interest that lasts at least two weeks.

Anger can be restrained or expressed openly. The level of anger and how it is conveyed differs from person to person.

You may also have other symptoms if you have depression. These are some examples:

- irritability
- loss of energy
- feelings of hopelessness
- thoughts of self-harm or suicide

Obsessive-compulsive disorder

Obsessive-compulsive disorder (OCD) is a type of anxiety illness marked by obsessive thoughts and compulsive activity. A person with OCD has unwelcome, unsettling ideas, desires, or visions that cause them to do something again and over again.

For example, people may do specific routines, such as counting to a number or repeating a word or phrase, because they have an illogical fear that if they don't, something horrible would happen.

Anger is a prevalent sign of OCD, according to a 2011 study. It affects almost half of all OCD sufferers.

Anger may arise as a consequence of irritation with your inability to control obsessive thoughts and compulsive activities or as a result of someone or something interfering with your capacity to perform a ritual.

Alcohol abuse

According to studies, drinking alcohol increases hostility. Alcohol is a factor in around half of all violent crimes perpetrated in the United States.

Alcohol abuse, often known as alcoholism, is defined as consuming an excessive amount of alcohol at once or regularly.

Alcohol inhibits your ability to think clearly and rationally. It affects your impulse control and can make it difficult to control your emotions.

Attention deficit hyperactivity disorder

ADHD is a neurodevelopmental disease characterized by symptoms such as inattention, hyperactivity, and/or impulsivity.

Symptoms typically appear in early childhood and persist throughout a person's life. Some people are not diagnosed with ADHD until they are adults, which is frequently referred to as adult ADHD.

Anger and irritability can develop in persons of all ages with ADHD. Other signs and symptoms include:

- restlessness
- problems focusing
- poor time management or planning skills

Oppositional defiant disorder

Oppositional defiant disorder (ODD) is a behavioral disorder that affects 1 to 16 percent of school-age children. Common symptoms of ODD include:

- anger
- hot temper
- irritability

Children with ODD are often easily annoyed by others. They may be defiant and argumentative.

Bipolar disorder

Bipolar disorder is a neurological illness that causes extreme mood swings.

These strong mood swings can range from mania to sadness, though depression does not affect everyone with bipolar illness. Many patients with bipolar disorder have episodes of fury, impatience, and anger.

During a manic episode, you may:

- be easily agitated
- feel euphoric
- have racing thoughts
- engage in impulsive or reckless behavior

During a depressive episode, you may:

- feel sad, hopeless, or tearful
- lose interest in things once enjoyed
- have thoughts of suicide

Intermittent explosive disorder

Intermittent explosive disorder (IED) is characterized by repeated episodes of aggressive, impulsive, or violent conduct. They may overreact to events by exploding in anger that is out of proportion to the situation.

Episodes last less than 30 minutes and appear out of nowhere. People suffering from the illness may be irritated and angry most of the time.

Some common behaviors include:

- temper tantrums
- arguments
- fighting
- physical violence
- throwing things

People with IED may feel remorseful or embarrassed after an episode.

Grief

One of the stages of grieving is anger. Grief can be caused by the death of a loved one, a divorce or breakup, or the loss of a career. The person who died, anyone else involved in the event, or inanimate objects may be the target of the rage.

Other symptoms of grief include:

- shock
- numbness
- guilt
- sadness
- loneliness
- fear

Anger issues symptoms

Anger results in both physical and emotional problems. While these symptoms are natural to encounter on occasion, a person with anger issues is likely to experience them more frequently and to a greater extent.

Physical symptoms

Anger has an impact on various aspects of your body, including your heart, brain, and muscles. According to a 2011 study, anger induces a rise in testosterone and a drop in cortisol levels.

The physical signs and symptoms of anger include:

- increased blood pressure
- increased heart rate
- tingling sensation
- muscle tension

Emotional

Several emotions go hand in hand with anger. You may notice the following emotional symptoms before, during, or after an episode of anger:

- irritability
- frustration
- anxiety
- rage
- stress
- feeling overwhelmed
- guilt

Anger issues types

Anger can manifest itself in several different ways. Not all anger is expressed in the same way. Anger and aggression can be outward, inward, or passive.

- **Outward**. This involves expressing your anger and aggression in an obvious way. This can include behavior such as shouting, cursing, throwing or breaking things, or being verbally or physically abusive toward others.
- **Inward**. This type of anger is directed at yourself. It involves negative self-talk, denying yourself things that make you happy, or even basic needs, such as food. Self-harm and isolating yourself from people are other ways anger can be directed inward.
- **Passive**. This involves using subtle and indirect ways to express your anger. Examples of this passive-aggressive behavior include giving someone silent treatment, sulking, being sarcastic, and making snide remarks.

Do I have anger issues?

You may have anger issues if:

- you feel angry often
- you feel that your anger seems out of control
- your anger is impacting your relationships
- your anger is hurting others
- your anger causes you to say or do things you regret
- you're verbally or physically abusive

Anger issues management

Consider seeking help from a mental health professional if you believe your anger is out of control or if it is negatively affecting your life or relationships.

A mental health expert can assist you in determining whether you have an underlying mental health disorder that is causing your anger issues and needs to be treated.

Anger management may also comprise one or more of the following strategies:

- relaxation techniques
- behavioral therapy
- depression, anxiety, or ADHD medications, if you're diagnosed with any of these conditions
- anger management classes, which can be taken in person, by phone, or online
- anger management exercises at home
- support groups

Chapter Three

The Effects of Poorly Managed Anger

Anger by itself isn't always a problem. Anger can be beneficial because it not only alerts us to difficulties in our lives that need to be addressed, but it can also inspire us to make those changes.

Connections Between Anger and Stress

When we are unduly stressed, we become more prone to anger, and both anger and stress become more difficult to handle. When the fight or flight reaction is activated and we become physiologically aroused as a result, we may become more readily enraged. Here are some of the reasons:

- When we are stressed, we are more likely to interpret a situation as threatening, which can easily lead to anger.
- When the fight or flight reaction is activated, we may not think as clearly or rationally, leaving us feeling less capable of managing.
- When the body's stress reaction becomes stimulated, emotions can escalate more quickly, leading to a quick temper.
- Factors that contribute to stress, such as risks to one's social position, emotional well-being, or simply having too many expectations, can all lead to anger.
- Anger and stress can feed off one other, so when we are anxious, we may get more easily angered, and poor reactions to anger can cause even more stress.

Challenges That Result From Poorly Managed Anger

Like poorly managed stress, anger that isn't handled healthily can be not only uncomfortable but even damaging to one's health and personal life. This can, of course, lead to greater levels of stress and anger. Consider the following research on anger:

- One study from the University of Washington School of Nursing studied anger problems in husbands and wives.1□ Researcher cited previous evidence that anger problems and depressive symptoms have been linked to all major causes of death. However, the women had a greater association between anger and symptoms of depression, while the men tended to experience an association between anger and health problems.
- According to a study from Ohio State University, those who had less control over their anger tended to heal more slowly from wounds.2□ Researchers gave blisters to 98 participants and found that, after 8 days, those who had less control over their anger also tended to be slower healers. In addition, those participants also tended to have more cortisol (a stress hormone) in their system during the blistering procedure, suggesting that they may be more stressed by difficult situations as well.
- Another study from the Harvard School of Public Health studied hostility in men and found that those with higher rates of hostility not only had poorer pulmonary functioning (breathing problems) but experienced higher rates of decline as they aged.3□
- Research with children and adolescents shows that anger management is important for the

younger set as well.4□ Findings showed that youth who cope inappropriately with their anger are at greater risk for problem-ridden interpersonal relationships. Their health is also at risk; those who cope poorly with anger tend to have more negative outcomes when it comes to both mental and general health. This highlights the fact that anger management is an important skill to learn early in life.

These are just a few of the numerous studies that relate anger to a variety of physical and emotional health issues, ranging from the apparent to the unexpected. Because badly managed anger is such a huge problem in so many areas of life, it's critical to take steps toward understanding and employing good anger management skills, as well as stress management techniques, in daily life.

It is critical to deal with anger healthily.

Managing Rather Than Ignoring Anger

Anger should be managed rather than suppressed or ignored since it can teach us what we want, what we don't want, and what we need to do next. Anger may be a valuable tool when viewed as a signal to pay attention to rather than a feeling to avoid or be embarrassed by. Listening to anger as a signal does not imply believing and acting on every angry idea or urge we have while we are enraged.

Uncontrolled anger might cause more problems than the circumstances that prompted it in the first place. When feelings of anger are mild, it is crucial to pay attention to them, understand where they are coming from, and rationally select the best course of action to follow to handle the anger and the situation that produced the anger. However, this is easier said than done.

Here are some things to keep in mind when dealing with anger.

1. Calm Your Body

When our anger is ignited, it's tempting to react in ways that aggravate the problem, whether that means saying things we'll later regret or taking reckless actions that may not consider all parts of a scenario. It is preferable to answer from a state of calm rather than from a state of wrath. This is why if at all possible, soothing your body and mind is a valuable first step in regulating anger.

Many stress management approaches, such as breathing exercises, short exercise, or even shifting your concentration for a few minutes to get distance from the triggering incident, can help with anger management (which is why counting to 10 has been recommended over the years as a first step before reacting when angry).

2. Identify the Cause of Your Anger

We often know what has made us angry, although this is not always the case. When we are angry, we are occasionally angry with something else, and the target we've picked is safer than the one who has made us angry (for example, when we are upset with someone who could hurt us, we take our wrath out on someone less dangerous).

Sometimes a lot of things have piled up, and the trigger of our anger is merely the straw that broke the camel's back. And occasionally the triggering incident has just tapped into some underlying unresolved anger that we've been carrying; this is frequently the case when our response appears disproportionate to the triggering event, especially when other stresses and triggers aren't present.

What You Can Do

It can be beneficial to write about your sentiments in a notebook until you feel clearer, chat to a close friend about your feelings and let them help you process your thoughts, or seek the support of a skilled therapist to help you understand the source of your anger. (You might also try a mix of all three.) These exercises can also aid with stress management, so it's a win-win situation.

3. Decide on a Course of Action

This time, you can enlist the help of a journal, a friend, or a therapist. Stress management techniques can also be useful in this situation. Techniques for shifting perspective, such as cognitive reframing, might help you look at things differently and possibly see something that makes you less irritated with the situation, or see answers that you may not have seen before.

Looking for other people's opinions can also be beneficial in terms of providing ideas for further actions to take as well as various points of view to see the situation differently, possibly in a less frustrating way. Using resilience-building stress management practices can also help you create emotional resilience, which can help with anger.

Know When to Seek Support

Some people have persistent anger issues, and others may find themselves in a circumstance that causes them to experience overpowering emotions. If you believe you could benefit from additional treatment with anger management, expressing your thoughts and feelings with a therapist can be incredibly beneficial, not just in addressing specific issues that cause anger, but also in developing a plan to handle anger and stress in the future. If you believe you require further assistance in regulating your anger, don't be hesitant to seek it.

CONCLUSION

Anger is a normal emotion, but if it appears out of control or is interfering with your relationships, you may have anger issues.

A mental health expert can assist you in working through your anger and identifying any underlying mental health disorders that may be a cause. You can control your rage using anger management and other treatments.